CREELAND

CREELAND

Dallas Hunt

NIGHTWOOD EDITIONS

2021

Nightwood Editions
P.O. Box 1779
Gibsons, BC VON 1VO
Canada
www.nightwoodeditions.com

COVER DESIGN: Anna Boyar
COVER AND AUTHOR PHOTO: Conor McNally
TYPOGRAPHY: Derek von Essen

Nightwood Editions acknowledges the support of the Canada Council for the Arts, the
Government of Canada, and the Province of British Columbia through the BC Arts Council.

This book has been produced on 100% post-consumer recycled, ancient-forest-free paper,
processed chlorine-free and printed with vegetable-based dyes.

Printed and bound in Canada.

LIBRARY AND ARCHIVES CANADA CATALOGUING IN PUBLICATION

Title: Creeland / Dallas Hunt.
Names: Hunt, Dallas, 1987- author.
Description: Poems.
Identifiers: Canadiana (print) 20200354647 | Canadiana (ebook) 20200354655 |
    ISBN 9780889713925 (softcover) | ISBN 9780889713932 (HTML)
Classification: LCC PS8615.U676 C74 2021 | DDC C811/.6—dc23

for nikâwiy

CONTENTS

my kôhkom could pick up a hatchet with her toes fell whole oaks
keep a fire for weeks trees speak to one another with vocabularies that
could burst the grammars that house us roots and tentacles spreading
reaching unfolding clasped branches like rough and clammy hands
searching for irriguous dirt crumbling like empires saplings could
topple empires if we would just get out of the way

CREE DICTIONARY

the translation for joy
in Cree is a fried bologna sandwich
the translation for bittersweet in Cree
looks like a cows and plows payment
eight decades too late
the translation for patience
in Cree is an auntie looking after four of her own children
and two of her sister's
the translation for evil
in Cree is the act of not calling
your mother on a Sunday

the translation for expedition
in Cree is travelling twenty minutes
to the only gas station in Faust, Alberta
to buy a Hygaard pizza sub
the translation for success in Cree
is executing the perfect frog splash
on your younger brother
the Cree word for white man is unpaid child support
the translation for conflicted in Cree
is your deep, steadfast love
for country superstar
Dwight Yoakam (or, depending on
the regional dialect,
George Jones, Patsy Cline
or Blue Rodeo)

the Cree word for constellation
is a saskatoon berry bush in summertime
the translation for policeman

in Cree is mîci nisôkan, kohkôs
the translation for genius
in Cree is my kôhkom muttering in her sleep
the Cree word for poetry is your four-year-old
niece's cracked lips spilling out
broken syllables of nêhiyawêwin between
the gaps in her teeth

LOUISE

nôhkom nitânskotapân
was born
with one
eye
and one
kid-
ney

for her grandchildren
she worked
her brittle fingers
into dough,
into the edges
of fires,
into frost-lined
canopies,
into dust she'd
knead with
flour and
bake for
us awâsisak

"bannock weighs
heavy on bones,"
she'd say,
and lick the
lard from fingers
that cracked with
love and life
for ancestors that

linger,
welcomely, and
for the
ancestors
to come

for white men,
nôhkom nitânskotapân
has awâs
tattooed on her
knuckles,
her back hunched,
vigilant, yet
carrying herself
with that
looseness of being
that glides on,
and with,
the wind

nôhkom nitânskotapân
strikes with the
fury of
a thousand
aunties,
whispering
"there is no
word for
benevolent
white men
in my
language"

KINANÂSKOMITIN

thank you
to the families
that feed us,
soft-footed near
traplines and
ambling for
treelines

thank you
for the hides
and dry sinew
that cracks between
teeth and gently
punctures the
skin

thank you
to all of the
wolf willows and pin
cherries that are
just trying
to make it
to autumn intact,
as we all
so often
are

and kinanâskomitinâwâw
to all
the uncles
that try
and the
aunties
that do

though, let's
be clear that
trying is
not the
same as
doing

DANCING YELLOW THUNDER

a shove off!
creaking clumsily on one foot,
followed haphazardly by the other, hang-
ing in time, your hips swinging,
staggering to a silence
that reverberates through
the hall.

your forehead gleaming with
sweat, mouth dry, parched, dancing
differently than what
fell from
elders' mouths.

your soft, worn hands grasp-
ing for the receiving hands of
a(n) (inviting) partner, the
lush manes of mares absent so
the wind obliges, whirling
you around, until
you lie splayed
on the legion
floor.

this is no sun dance, but
you tap your toes in time with
the tsk tsks, thrust into a
dance from oblivion, a void with
no history, another Indian emerging
from the earth, steeped in mutilated
self-worth, motivated, they'll say, by
endless, endless thirst.

next time, i will dance with
you, Raymond, and we
will stomp our boots so
hard we'll create sparks that
rise to the heavens, that
call forth clouds and yellow
thunder, and we will watch as ·
they do the electric boogaloo—
the smell of singed hair
filling
the hall.

NO OBVIOUS SIGNS OF DISTRESS

in Canada, what came first,
the prison cell or the casket?

colonialism is waiting
eighteen hours in a cell
when you desperately
need a hospital,

is when you(r) burst
blood vessels are read
as a night on the town.

an RCMP officer is
a prison guard is
a school teacher is
a hospital where
you are
sterilized
unknowingly.

your body is
described,
rendered
as "collapsed,"
"slumped,"
burdened by descriptors so
loaded
that they
undermine the
sympathy

they are
purported to
garner.

settler colonialism
is not
the
fear
of dying
but "the fear
of dying
alone."

an expert
testifies,
speaks strongly
to how
these conditions
are opposed to
"operating procedures,"
to a past perfect:
mistakes *had been* made,
not that they are, and will be
made
again, in perpetuity.

it's hard
for institutions
to respond to
medical crises
when medical
crises

are how they're
constituted.

basically what they
produce
and how
you are
produced
when "impaired"

suspends

care,
even though being "impaired"
is when one
actually might
need
care.

a
"disorienting
event"
exacerbated
by the police
leaves you
forever changed
when life
itself
isn't over
but "the life
you knew
is."

a brain
perforated
a chronic limp
a stark
message that
being "detained"
or containment
is the essence
of your existence
in these spaces,
as though detainment
is supposed to feel
like a welcoming
blanket
wrapped
around
a mallet
meant to
pulverize,
like
they "stole four and a half years"
of your life
because routine
check-ups
and adequate
items for
sleep
are not needed
cause they
never work
and, rarely,
if ever,

work as
well,
or feel
as good
to *them*
as a mallet
will.

my kôhkom's rib-cage plumage wrapped around a plum skeleton of barbed wire and electricity bones that catch in the throat of those that wish any of her grandchildren ill cartilage that bends but doesn't break bends and bends and bends until the slack tightens up and slaps white men in the face cumulus cloud that rumbles grey battering the side of houses gale winds that utter Cree like a caress and a threat (whisper like a brick wall) astam if you know what's good for you

ADA STREET, POCATELLO

fashion shifts,
silk trades end

the (colonial) gateway
to the northwest

a benevolent misnomer
Portneuf Gap more of a maw

listed under services:
park pavilions, dumpsters

banks of mink,
cities of daisies

every road and website ends
in a 502 gateway

balled and burlapped,
with soil covering the root flare

leaves like lightning
clusters hanging

tree guides with
soft but stern subheadings:

prohibited as street trees,
trees with significant problems

and near the index,
recommended shrubs

a cut across
the sky

spatter chaperoned,
snaking to your slight feet

bundled, housed in a smile
capital

sawabi: the word
for sagebrush

MAHIHKAN

wolf bones
are tender,
he said, and
in that moment
i believed him.

we exited
the vehicle,
amazed at the
travelling container of
release and ruin that
we had been
riding in. Kia
is Korean for
murder, he joked.
i didn't laugh.

somewhere
behind the thickets,
nestled between shrubs
and budding Jack pines,
lay wolf pups,
wondering where their mother
was and where
this ache had
come from.

rarely do you see
wolves by
the highway,
i say, and for a moment
it looks like
he might believe me.

we trudge through
the snow back
to the compact
car with the
leather interior—
it was a rental.

WAHKOHTOWIN

on our

window-
sill

        sits
           a succulent,
                bending

            its stem

                        to swallow
                    the sunlight

hunched over,
      desperate,
           it leans toward
              the glass,
                    hoping
                to be filled
                  like a
       Mason jar
           brimmed by
              a pouring
                  spout—
                    before
                        the

water
      rushes over

how wonderful

                              to be so
                              dependent
                                          on another, how

            alarming, how
terrifying

                              and yet,
                                    what else is

                                                there to do,
            but to have
                        our beings
bound up
in others,

                                    so restless, so
            full

of
thirst

                        that
                        we might

                                    spill over

HEALING, SUSPENDED

healing: if not
now, then
when?
sentiment
appreciated, but
the inverse is
also true—

death: if
not now,
then when?
if
release is
taboo, then
when can i
make room,
plant seedlings,
feed
through
digestive
tissue,
wild strains
wisping,
whipping in
the wind

i read
that a teenager
spent seven
months hanging
from a tree,
less than
thirty kilometres,
and more than half
a year (in)voluntarily
removed,
from/into "care"

until a blade,
serrated edge,
sunders, kisses
twine: if not
now—his family,
his community,
grief asks—then
when?

i keep
circling back
to this,
because
what if
the only

time one is
free is when
one stakes a
claim to
a space
between
earth and
the sky, to
suspended
relief

when tall
grass tickles
toes, when one's
kin carries
weight
better than
institutions created
for your "well-being"
do—
ones that
frame freedom as
an empty hotel
room, as
[permanent]
staycation, as
weekend get-
away

an elder tells
me that an
old burial rite
was to place
one's body
at the top of a tree,
so i convince
myself you
wanted to
see everything,
the apex of
a pine tree,
prairie stretching
in perpetuity,
prairie chickens
preening

freezing
faces, snot
sticking to
the peeling
raw
bottoms of
nostrils,
wind chill besieging:
if not
now, then
when?

TRACKS

if birds left   tracks
in the   sky they'd
look like   fault lines
scuttling   friction
heat   leaking
the sky   spilling
over

if birds left   tracks
in the sky   huddles disrupted
clouds frustrated   schemes
half-cooked   i hope they find
a means to
end us   anyhow

if birds   left,
right now   while the getting
bears fruit   there
might be   hope
for them   yet,
keep   your migration
patterns   a secret:
we deserve   this.

if birds left   we'd all
feel less   guilty,
you ever   see
a flashbulb   swallowed,
a kiss   blown
in a   tsunami?

34

if birds left   i'd wish
them a safe   journey
Noah   adrift
at sea   all in all
better   that way—
okay   less biblical:

if birds   left   they'd
be righteous   justified
an unspoken   promise
ended

if birds left   now
before   the grim reapers arrive
and came back   when it was
over,   then
it might   all be worth it

I WAS BORN BLUE

umbilical cord
caressing,
a hug a
trimester
too long,
attached
at the neck
my mother hugging
me to death
before
she knew—
before she
met me

a C-section
is a bursting forth
into the world,
flitting through
uterine lining,
birth by cut,
cut cut   c   u t
an excision

i came into
the world,
not thrashing,
nor crying,
but with lips
pursed, an echo,
half whimper,

lingering ultrasound,
a referent with
no reference,
dangling
modifier,
all body,
no presence

a friend
of mine relayed to
me that
when you're born
blue it means
you were in
the womb too long,
gripping your mother,
anatomies
of comfort,
until history arrives
on your doorstep
provides context,
a birth
alert, if you live
in the Prairies
(one must
always be alert
in the Prairies)

when you're born
blue, odds are you've
defecated in the womb
been birthed alongside

fecal matter,
shit your first friend,
an odious
comrade-
in-arms

when you're born
blue you
cling to
big-belly kinship
you risk your life
to be closer to your mother
since you know you'll
never have
this closeness again

it was worth it,
being born blue,
to be outside
of history
for a moment,
to relate deeply
to a mother
who will not have
the vocabularies
to relate
to you otherwise
in the future

maybe being born blue
was the happiest
time in your life,

excrement your blanket
waiting to meet kikâwiy
before history rushes in,
pours over,
like a nursery
of fire,
cruel smelting,
lava slowly
encroaching

she'll do her best,
and yet (to them)
that will never be
enough

SCRAPS FROM SUMMER VISITS

when i was eight years old

my cousin asked
me, earnestly,

did our ancestors
wish on shooting stars?

soft-serve ice cream
from the egg fair,
the taste of
cold cream
in our
mouths

do our ancestors wish
on shooting stars?

he asked the
following summer
i shrugged,
changed
the subject,
but wanted to
tell him

so lucky are
we that
the moon
loves us
all

next summer,
Inglewood,
a row of townhouses,
Northside of
Edmonton,
my cousin
staying with us
for four days,
spending
most of
that time
in his
gonchies,
stated
to me plainly,
self-assured,

our ancestors
are shooting stars.

RUEFUL

for Doris

our apartment
smells like onions
in the way
a grandmother does,
like the back
of a prune-soaked
hand—
a cartography
of swollen
lines and
deep
creases

he stands
on his hind legs,
gulping, eyes
bulging, desperate,
communicating

the news cycle
is exactly that—
recursive, numbing.
headlines read:

"this world is one that insists
on constant bruising
and yet adamantly encourages us
not to be tender.
that is to say, it asks us to house
bruises, but not the way
a bruise feels"

a world unto itself, ignorant
a constellation collapsing, beguiled

i want more than
what
this world
can give me.
i want to flourish,
be mirthful, to burn
down a bank, hi-
jack a Tesla,
preferably with
Elon Musk
in the passenger seat

as i swerve
into a rock bed
what does it mean to be tender?

desire, tentative:
to hear
your voice and
your voice
only

tender like your vocal cords
straining, stretching,
a voice overburdened,
quivering

the last time
i saw my
grandmother
she lay on
a cot next to
the freezer,
dying of
cancer

the deep-freeze
she'd rustle
around in
when we
were children,
digging deep
to find us
stray freezies,
and freezer-burnt
popsicles
with sticky
wrappers

the last time
i saw my grandmother,
we travelled
330 kilometres to
watch her die,
all knowingly.
her body
in revolt,
with her
unable to
explain or
articulate
how or
why

a body tender and
still betrayal

the last time
i saw my grandmother
i could
see creases:
the world
nestled
in the back of
her hands,
layers
unfurling

like an onion

her cot
a map
of the world,
her death
the north
folding in
on itself

propped
on her elbow
at a forty-five-degree
angle, stripping an
orange of its
rind, at
once violent
and tender

150 KILOMETRES WEST OF SASKATOON

for Colten Boushie

dust kicks
up as the
axle bears
the weight of
a creaky under-
carriage,
and
small pebbles
smack, relentlessly,
against the
windshield

you, sun-soaked, glistening,
sit with the water still
running
off the tips
of your
thin fingers, a
welcome
friend when the grass
yellows and quivers,
a spark to
start it
all

how could you
possibly know that
he was
simmering,
like a frog
in boiling
water, or a
toad
set to bake
at one thousand
eight hundred and
seventy-six
degrees Celsius

how could you know
that, careless,
armed
with history,
and buoyed
by popular opinion,
he would
cast his
hate forward,
unable to breathe
under
all that
counterfeit
prairie hospitality

and how could you
possibly know
that so many were
unable to attend
to the
idea
that you
could be
human,
too

SMALL

i used to not
like to be made
to feel small

but now,
i like it down
here with

the mulch,
ladybugs,
loam; the sticks.

aphids in
arms, hand
in hand

with the mites
and gnats,
mycologist in

miniature,
fungi my
friends.

i'm happy,
now, in my studies,
to gaze upward,

to scheme,
plan tactics,
nascent strategies,

to set the stage,
if you will,
for alimentary outbreaks.

mushrooms and me
blueprints in tow,
toxic cocktails of aleukia

at the ready.
yes, i don't mind
feeling small

'cause you can
see, and plot,
a lot from down here.

STRETCH MARKS // SUN DOGS

i dream that
the sun is my
fat-bodied kin

glowing, their smile
blanching earth yellow—
beach sands,
setting my chubby cheeks
ablaze

we embrace,

swollen,
sweaty, full
of love,
malevolent light
languishing &
strolling
across chunky
appendages
stretch marks & sun dogs,

accomplices
in bulbous joy,
me reeling as
pîsim's luminous
touch
collides
with my
perfectly
un-moisturized
skin

they smile

and,
beneath pîsim's grin,
mouth piquing,
crowded
by freckles and
insurgent
moles,
i smile with them

THE CREE WORD FOR CAREENING

thin air during the day,
prior to 4:30 p.m.

i am a particle
dust dispersed,
stars the mother
i'll never see again
diaspora my clinking bones

my teeth are
galaxies, asteroids
clambering together,
my molars the
afterlives of
solar flares

the freeing residues
of stars letting go
of being undone—
what else is there
to do when you're
a star, but let go?

i am the rising
tides, the moon's
orbit my waistline,
flooding is love
(to be) made in
overflowing, pipes
bursting

a comet
with no end,
in a word:
intergalactic.
a shooting
star crestfallen
and plummeting.
faint, fatigued
and regretful

but willing to fall
again

what's the Cree word
for careening?

WOMAN MAKING TEA

for Annie Pootoogook

you hold tight
to a
single
hanging
slingshot, to protect
against
the flash-
bulbs
and negligent
headlines

deadwood leaves
shine light
where safe
shadows
harbour
those fleeing
heavy hands

writers' deadlines
complicit in flat-
lines, food lines,
procession
lines—
looking for but
unseeing the
scoop(s)

gawking, with
the death of print
culture weighing
heavy, benefit
from the benefits that
keep the
taste of
perfect teeth
in their
mouths

seeing your photo now,
appreciating
the gentle shadings
of your eyebrows and
the cracks that
line your face
lines that
hold
constellations and
such small,
ordinary gifts
that you
gave to
us all

MOZART, SASKATCHEWAN

a white man is a fist
that ends
families, that
destroys worlds,
a blizzard
in dry summer.
a white man is shitty
birthday gifts, a
reused holiday card,
a call eight days after
Christmas, a misspelled
personalized key chain.
a white man is a mouth full
of cavities, 'cause he doesn't know
where the nearest dentist is
and he doesn't care.
a white man is a tornado
in Edmonton in 1987,
flattening the northeast side
of a city,
clustered power
flashes,
beaming
and dissipating
as quickly as he arrived.
a white man coaxes,
he throws down
stairs, hurls
against
walls, pounds

against the earth,
with (others')
extremities.
a white man is a fist,
illiterate
and still
makes more money
than kikâwiy, despite
being half
as smart
and nowhere
near as talented.
a white man is dirty
knuckles, fading
and smudged
black Sharpie
filling the creases
of his taut
backhand,
an amateur
graffiti artist, writing
epithets in
bathroom
stalls,
in blue
Bic ballpoint pen.
a white man is your weight
gain, your overworked heart
ventricles, stilted
emotions, your stifled
speech,
an adult

stutter.
a white man is a fist,
he will outlive you
by two decades
and be
celebrated
for it—
"it's always
a shame,"
he crows,
"to outlive
your children"—
and he
will cry
at your
wake,
sombre,
uninvited,
but relieved,
at peace,
and full
of cheer.

CHRIS GAINES

someone needs
to write a poem
on how Garth Brooks'
Chris Gaines
persona was
an expression of
radical vulnerability,
but one that
was immediately
stamped out by
the imposed and
imposing dictates
of cis-heteronormative
masculinity

but yes,
the soul
patch was
a bad
idea

1. the dollar store down the street in Kitsilano sells ninety-eight-cent abalone shells with maple leaves stickered all over them. heal me

2. i don't want to be cremated. just place my corpse in Fort Edmonton Park so some unsuspecting settler can find me and i can ruin their day

3. fireworks are explosions; they disrupt networks of kin, hurt birds and perforate my dog's eardrums

4. settler colonialism. *See* "the crime you see now, it's hard to even take its measure"

5. a thing i'm rationally afraid of: the raised voice of an entitled white man

6. multi-generational hurts are also fireworks; they paint an endless black expanse, bleed against a backdrop before fading into it; they are graffitied pain

7. i keep mistakenly reading "self-isolation" as "self-immolation"

8. occupation: a hoarse whisper, an accusation unevenly distributed and yet true nonetheless, a faculty lunch conversation best avoided

9. i'll eat Stove Top stuffing every day of the year, until sodium fills my lungs and my heart implodes, before i'll celebrate thanksgiving earnestly

10. March 12, 2020: i read that Justin Trudeau "self-isolated" and i let out a soft, involuntary moan

11. a fictive coherence. *See* Canada; a *Globe and Mail* comments section; life as deferral, as survival with an open invitation toward death

12. i wish i cared about anything as much as white people care about toilet paper

13. my white grandfather lived and settled on the lands my Cree great-grandfather gave up so his daughter wouldn't have to attend residential school

14. Sir John A. Macdonald was a drunken white supremacist, something i'll scream into the soft arches of your feet as they press into my temples

15. a niece of mine was born so premature that my mother described her as being so small that you could fit her in your hand like a pound of butter

I ONLY TRIED TO BREAK

nôhtâwiy is a knock
at the door best left

unanswered. His ancestors a bruising
cacophony, fists pelting hardwood,

brutal messiahs demanding
entry, their histories a battering

ram, a cleaving through fragile door frames.
He clamours, "I only tried to break

the door down to make a stone
out of you." Chert, most likely,

a set of stress, thrust faulting, a focal point
of pressurized slamming, deadbolts crumbling.

nôhtâwiy is a rap(ture) at the door,
a grim reaper in FILA track pants.

I yell from the other side,
"I only want to be the air that slips

between the gaps in your fingers,"
those eager hands quietly forming

heavy fists. My peephole a glimpse
into weathering debris. The debris he'll make

out of me. Deposition, the ebb and flow
of small particles, until sedimentation

occurs and I'm at the bottom
of an estuary, water passing over, gliding

and soothing, carrying wounds to still
lakes and crummy ponds.

my kôhkom has a fist like a claw-foot pedestal cast-iron fingernails a gallop-like gait horseshoes for teeth so when the air pushes through incisors a warning siren whistles like a death knell your bulldozer stops here have this conservation area west of your region on the one hand clear-cut the other to the east effluvium and detritus finding a home in an estuary until she inhales all that waste and deposits it at your dinner party in your quinoa salad

A PRAIRIE FIRE THAT WANDERS ABOUT

for Treaty Eight

when you arrive

        dust

and dirt commingle

        petals of

larkspur

        and black knot

fill lungs

        choke seedlings

annual wildfires

        clear the rest.

home is a nest

        burrowed in the arms

of cygnets

        on the one hand

and in the

        teeth of a

nodding donkey

        on the other—

reciprocal

        kitchen-table kinship

and reciprocating

        piston pumps

"this is how

        we live here,"

questions

        unwelcome.

every auntie

        in Treaty Eight

hugs the

    same way

thank(s)

      god.

it's only three

    hours away

from Edmonton

    if you drive fast

enough, and depending

    on what

you're running

    from. welcome.

i hope to die

    here, a place

i've been running from

    my whole life

and yet whose grip

    carries my imagination

and whose

    landscapes i've been

preparing to be

    buried in, if

i'm lucky,

    my whole life.

"bury me in

    clear-cut territories,"

in hurts that

    nourish. there's

no place to

    eat sleep eat

otherwise.

    i am here

i shout to

                                     no one

and no one

                                     minds

home is when

                                     no one realizes

when you're here

                                     and no one

notices

                                     when you leave.

the clouds here

                                     are bigger than

anywhere else in

                                     the world, they

nestle and hail

                                     they blanket my

face with gentle stones

                                     accost me until

i know,

                                     consent,

and

                                     agree,

that i will

                                     perish here,

a muddy

                                     puddle off

Highway 2.

MAIN STREET AND SIXTH AVENUE

There's a 7-Eleven
in Slave Lake
with the best potato wedges
and chicken wings in
all of what is
currently called
North America

When you discard
the freshly
stripped chicken
wings, pigeons
pick at and fight
over the bones
while seagulls
swallow them
whole

Is it cannibalism
when birds
eat each other's
bones?
The 7-Eleven sits
at the intersection
of Main Street

and Sixth Avenue,
an area touched
by the tips
of flames
but not engulfed
by them

Half of Slave Lake
burned down in 2011,
with Fort McMurray
following a few years
later. The sentiment
at the time was
not to critique
the resource extraction
industry—people
had lost their
homes, after all

But it was
precisely at
these moments
that the tar sands,
and extractivism,
should have been
at the forefront of
conversations

A palpable climate
of loss, anger,
helplessness
and rage in the
air, hanging
like acrid
black smoke
blanketing a
lush forest
(recently
designated for
clear-cutting)

There are discrete,
temporary, but possibly
incredibly generative
moments to mobilize
affect in Northern Alberta
that do not revolve around
the looming busts of
the oil field or a
Connor McDavid
shooting slump—
but instead, wildfires,
misused funds, a
funeral
gone wrong

The next time a
prairie fire threatens
to inhale a Northern Alberta
hamlet or
municipality, we need
to foreground the
resource extraction
industry, we need to
kick down the doors
of oily-haired CEOs
and parade them through
the wide,
unpaved streets
of the north,
and dip the tops
of their heads in
the spiking
flames, the wide
maw of the inferno

We need to treat
them like a seagull
treats a recently
discarded
chicken-wing
bone

A CROOK THAT SIGNIFIES HOME

i read an article
on the CBC today
that declared that
"Arthritis affects
Indigenous people at a rate
three times higher
than average"

i wonder what it
means when trauma
makes a house with/in
your bones, when
marrow is sweet
with the
tongues and
acimowin of
your kin,
obliterated
by the intense
yet boring
mechanisms
that make
an endoskeleton
creak

i wonder too
what it means
to have diabetes
in a food desert
that settler

colonialism is a mirage,
a bad dream
of unpotable
water, a
nightmare only
fit to drink
if it is
boiled

i wonder what
it means to
go to a therapist
and have them
ascribe your
fury to
FASD,
to diagnose
relatives,
in absence,
as vessels
marred by,
and carrying
with/in them
spirits that
harm, that
overdetermine
through
bodily and
facial
tics or
"abnormalities"

i wonder what
it's like to be
fat and free
of disease
and insulin
injections,
to have a
thin upper
lip, stiff
from having
to answer
inane questions
from invasive
"healers," to
treat wide-set
eyes as
a gift
from your
ancestors

i wonder
what it is
like to not
have a predetermined
bundle of
signifiers rest
heavily on one's
shoulders,
to be able
to shrug off
an entire
discursive field

built on/off
the rigid but
brittle backs
of your
relatives,
that the
crook in your
kôhkom's
neck comes
from carrying
so many
little ones,
marked
the moment
they take in
that first
breath,
pushing the
air back
out,
through
their already
arthritic
bones

The definition of *spiral* is the paradoxical "winding around a centre or pole and gradually receding from or approaching it"—a spiral can recede and expand simultaneously, as long as the point of origin remains the same. When one spirals, though, it never looks like this; it's like a neutron star imploding, self-immolation magnified, skin tenderly separating from bone. It's a sense of hopelessness that doesn't feel like anything at all, except maybe like a gunshot wound in the chest with no exit wound or point of entry. It's ordering pizza and hot wings at three in the morning and sleeping in until two p.m. because you hate yourself. It's drinking alone, especially at a place called Jagger's Sports Bar, 'cause you can just show up, and, while everyone won't always know your name, they won't care to ask either. It's a place where you can sit next to someone and they, clad in dusty denim jacket, can implore, "BUT I AM ALONE, TOO. I AM LONELY, TOO!" You hear them, but avoid eye contact.

Spiralling is when you wish someone would bust a beer bottle over your head, but you drink alone, and there's no one there to oblige you, so instead you listen to your favourite Cat Power song at four a.m. and cry into the snot-stained sleeve of your favourite sweatshirt, or watch your favourite video of amateur choreography set to a Kehlani song. Spiralling is when, with greasy fingers, you order from Santa Lucia for the fourth time this week, and afterwards while trying to tie your shoes, you sweat into your eyes and your chest cavity clenches around your heart like a fist—that is to say, your body mobilizes, completely out of your control. Spiralling is realizing you can't enjoy eating out in public because you're fat and people snicker, stare or judge—you, trying to stake a claim to space, but doing it limply while they dismiss you anyway. Spiralling is going to a New Year's Eve party and cutting your stiff drink of gin with more gin, puking up the curry chicken you had the night before. It's spending a year cultivating a friendship and ruining it in an evening.

Spiralling is knowing you don't have mastery over your own consciousness, and it will sleep when it wants to, sanity a wager, with you desperately waiting to hit on the turn. Spiralling is starting your PhD and drinking yourself numb until you have vertigo, stumbling into the nearest casino across the Cambie Bridge—a place where everyone is lonely, too, desperately avoiding eye contact. Spiralling is when you exceed yourself and recede into yourself at the same time, your body convulsing, involuntarily crumbling until it's the size of a vervain hummingbird egg. Spiralling is knowing you're akin to the fastest bird on the planet according to this analogy, yet (the) slow (creep of) death catches up to you anyhow.

I ALMOST HAD A MENTAL BREAKDOWN DURING MY MASTER'S DEGREE

but it's not what you think:
it was quotidian, daily life
the everyday.

then came the fruit
flies:
                                              they cling.
                                          clung to the fan
                                      above the stovetop,
                                        withered banana
                                                    skins,
                                              Tupperware
                                                      seal
                                              half-cracked
they were everywhere
in the way
a mind is
when it approaches
its end
                                                 in short,
                                                i needed
                                                 to know
                                                  what to
                                                       do

i read a
mom blog
that said to mix
a Malbec
with dish soap,

and to cover
the lips
of a wineglass
with
saran wrap,
gentle
piercings
that swallow like
open manholes
littering
the top,
this would trap the flies
slow asphyxiation
three days
pass:

                                           the flies
                                                  still
                                                live in
                                        my territory,
                                        rent-free

in the corner
of my basement
suite, i find
a spider,
reason with
it silently:

                                         "hug the inside
                                      of the wineglass,
(diplomacy)   so that when
                                        the fruit fly
                                      tentatively
                                      enters through

the saran wrap,
it will be exposed,
a sacred meal"

(abject exposure)

in my mind,
this makes sense,
a deal done, a
spit-soaked
handshake

i lift the saran
wrap, dump
the spider in,
gleefully expecting
my kin   (kohkominaw)
to stick to
the side of
the translucent
container
with one leg,
and grab the fly
with the other—

                                                this is a
                                    conversation unhad, a
                                         plan unhatched

the spider slowly,
gradually,
painfully, begins
to slide
in the direction
of the
cocktail of

seventeen-
dollar Malbec
and certain
death
i've engineered

the still
current of
sour grapes
and
Palmolive
too strong
for eight
limber legs
to push
through,
to kick
toward   a glass shoreline
unreached

my best friend
the spider
tumbles into
the top
layer of dish
soap before
it hits the wine,
its trajectory
a crawl
in slow
motion

shaking tarsus
floats above
thick inebriant,
sinking,
and,
eventually,
dying,
my relation
slips to their
cherry-
plum-raspberry
acrid death

to make Malbec
you need to nurture
grapes,
shield them
from frost,
canopy growth,

and unruly high yields
the last thing
you want is a
Malbec of good
colour but
tannic in
nature, so
they say

Argentina
is one of
the largest
producers of
Malbec,
and i hope,
if i can bear
the flight path,
and my mind is
clear, then
i'll go there someday:
Malbec for a
heavy heart's
content,
hopeful
remedy
for swelling
grief

i leave before
the fruit flies
do

there are no good settlers, because settler colonialism is a structural relation that abdicates and ignores healthy ways of relating to one another. there are no good relations within asymmetrical relations of occupation, settlement and domination. until these problems are engaged with in a meaningful manner, the possibility of so-called good relations is an impossibility—settler colonialism, or coloniz-ation, forecloses good relations. of course, these are hard conversa-tions to have: no one wants to think of themselves as a bad relation. but until these violent systems are done away with, you're the uncle at a birthday party that keeps to himself, brings no presents, and drunkenly chews out his sisters midway through the gifting process. no doubt that this applies to the ways settlers learn the discourses of our dispossession and deploy them for their own means. what does it mean to one day randomly proclaim oneself Indigenous without the obligations such a designation entails, to then use, instrument-alize and mobilize harmful colonial policies as a way to absolve oneself from responsibilities, as though violence relinquishes one's responsibility to act ethically in a relational sense. when calculated claims to a marginalized identity buttress one's ability to avoid cri-tique, to prevent further inquiry, to relegate questioners to the realm of violence, this is, in fact, violence: especially since relational inquiry is how we establish who we are and how we are in relation to one another. in fact, institutions, both professional and artistic, are woe-fully unprepared to "designate" one as Indigenous, to "administer" one's Indigeneity, to decide if one is "Indigenous enough" for a title or position. you see, these conversations are difficult to have in a critical or institutional context, but perhaps a poetics of accountability can allow us to see each other differently, to speak knowingly and to discern when someone means well but is just a well-meaning white settler with no claim to Indigeneity, aside from the fact that it will help them in this institutional moment, when before this moment an Indigenous name was a death sentence, a job impediment.

in short, glad you "found" your Indigeneity, but that didn't prevent ndns from eating fried bologna sandwiches for eight years because no one would hire our mothers for meaningful (read: not menial) labour. stakes are everything, and without them, one can circulate as "an Indigenous expert," but you will never be invited to the kitchen table by the aunties, because they'll solve you quicker than a Rubik's Cube. incidents like settler self-Indigenization incite aunties to designate white people as the descendants of vultures, ones who circle and observe, until the carcass of Indigeneity is consumed, slurped up through ravenous beaks, and you attend your next Christmas dinner elaborating the plight of ndns, while we help our mothers steal a turkey from Safeway so our grandmothers and cousins can eat. so we can be together, picking bones clean, purposefully, leaving little, so vultures remain malnourished and starving in the process; an embarrassment, really, until another carcass floats, vulnerably, on small nourishing waves, on the water we've used for millennia to warn each other about you.

the future
is a ghost
you inherit,
close your
blinds before
bed, the future
will make
a mess of
you anyhow

hot breath,
the back of
goose-pimpled
necks, a
Dyson hand
dryer in
a public washroom,
i'd feel more at
home if
geese
weren't
such
assholes

eyeballs twitching
pressure mounting
like someone
placed a stack
of nickels behind
your orbital lobe,

orbital bone,
frontal cortex,
a brewing storm—
the creeping
feeling that
you're
lost
at sea

i'll find out
what's wrong
with me someday:
as my therapist
repeats, "it's
okay to be
anxious,
it's okay,
really,
to be
alive"

hark!, if
i'm lost
at sea
i hope
Willem
Dafoe is
there,
to comfort
me, i hope
to be

his understated
performance
in *The Florida
Project*,
(all) subtlety and
teeth,
perceptible
only to
lost ships
and lapping
waves

or not:
flatulence
my anchor,
my port a
poem, an
incomprehensible
mist,
directing,
until the
tide
flushes me
away,

again
and again

SPILLIMACHEEN

yes, predictably,
this poem is about
yearning—
desire: a longing
open toward wounding.
oriented toward
and against wounding.
constant wounding.
affect unmuted.
play. fun. joyful wounding.

the hard part of writing poetry
is when you can't
say anything.
when your stomach is empty.
when love falls apart,
refracts like light through a prism.
when love, mangled, refracted, stares
you in the eyes.
when you feel unmade
but love demands more,
interrogates—
who are you to deny me?
who are you
to demand
more
of me?

COMFORT

nothing ever feels good
when you're diagnosed as
crazy.   feels nothing.
a running litany of things
i'm irrationally afraid of:
      unidentified sounds
      being raptured
      reciprocating love
      becoming a serial killer
      hugs that linger
      my teeth falling out
      fruit flies
      feeling better
what if in the attempt
to flourish we throw
surviving out the window
off the Lion's Gate Bridge
down chasms
what if at the bottom
of a chasm is where
intimacy lies
don't think i'll survive
      the plunge
         baby
            with

bathwater
i've gained
weight, so a friend
asks me if i remember
when i used to have
cheekbones
          i don't, but

                    i hope to someday smile
like i do

EVEN TOMBS DIE

every ndn
knows another
ndn named Johnny—
this is no
exaggeration.
by my count,
there are probably
a thousand people
in Treaty Eight alone
named Johnny

when Jack Nicholson
bellowed, "Here's
Johnny!"
was that a
rez interpellation?
did he know that
ndns love games
of chance?

like crazy eights,
or a tennis
ball bouncing
softly,
between
bruises,
cracks in the
sidewalk, bricks
washed and
receding,

weathered
stones—
your môsom dies
before he can
teach you
how to play
crib

let's play
war,
you say,
but then you're
blamed
for rendering
us gambling
spirits, instigators
and recipients
of military violence,
pasts
haunting
iridescent futures:
malfunctioning
slot machines
with fifteen free
plays remaining

a ghost
bartender is
what my uncle
calls a Tuesday,
or a smudge
gone wrong—

how often
do they smudge
the River Cree
anyway

the Overlook
Hotel is built on the
remains of a thousand
dead ndns, on
a pulsating
burial ground,
on the back of a
thousand Johnnys,
ghouls palpitating

and yet,
ndn life
thrives
in the gaps
between
Letterman's
malocclusion,
teeming
in the traces
left by
Carson's
slur(red)
speech,
in the absences
of Kubrick's

punitive
lens,
in the
static,
white noise:

a breeding
ground for
cacophonous
and unruly
ghosts—
grief making a home
out of blunt teeth

WAKE

doubt is an ocean
a vast, capacious
body

your unwashed
ancestors traversed

the ocean mediates
seemingly ceaseless plateau
ships and their shameful bellies

underbellies and undercurrents
idiots at the helm

"once more unto the breach,"
your great-grandfather said
like a fucking idiot who'd
later go on to cannibalize

a village, settlement violently
arranged, a schema

did your ancestors bellow
"we the north"
unironically?
the bush rending
their flesh from bone

stripping bark to
weave a basket

let's picnic,
with this bounty
full of
plump hearts,
the fruit from
your family
tree

your ancestors had wooden teeth
(read: a mouth full of splinters)

is that a metaphor for
colonialism? probably,
or maybe your ancestors
should have brushed
their fucking teeth

there are miles at stake!
there are miles at stake!

a breaststroke
across the Atlantic
with nothing but
miles at stake

CURRICULUM IN THE WAIT

their bodies are open
their channels are open
this world is opening up
—Daughters, "Satan in the Wait"

every ndn novel
is about residential schools:
   did you hear, they're opening up?
   intentions be damned
   we need to find a frame,
   hurry, to hang legibility
   on the wall

every ndn poem
is about residential schools:
   the future is a pinhole
   eager tunnel to the past
   most visions double
   as tunnels
   why not the present?

every ndn play
is about residential schools:
   interpretation a crawl space
   history the asbestos
   damp, dirty drywall
   pooling at the bottom
   of your heavy, hardened lungs

every ndn memoir
is about residential schools:
   voice ringing across history
   a wavelength insisting
   "there's a tombstone where your headboard used to be!"
   "there's a——stone where your head———used to be!"
   "there's a tomb——where you———used to be!"

every ndn story
is about residential schools:
   did you know the
   growth of a hermit crab
   depends on the
   size of its shell?
   at risk of being eaten
   unless it can fully
   retract into it.
   did you know
   an ill-fitting
   shell is consignment
   to death?

NÎKÂNIHK

land and
landless,
what Wilderson III
dubs as "off
the
record"

a seemingly
unnavigable terrain,
a gap
impossible
to traverse—
combined futures
unimaginable

shutter resurgence
for a "radical antagonistic
project of abolition,"
for what other
alternatives could
there be?

but what of
the original
intent
of treaties?

that moment of possibility—
no matter
how
violent its
later, latter,
trailing
effects and
affects

what possibilities
here
to bridge
Octavia Butler
and Helen
Haig-Brown,
criss-
crossing futurities
that obliterate
white supremacy
and its many
sticky, stymying
resi-
dues?

futures whose
formation(s)
make another
one hundred and

fifty years impossible,
that eclipse
an actively
erasing history
of white
men wearing
ill-fitting
toupées

and that
keep terrible
white men in
the past, awful
môniyâwak
not even
fit
to be
ghosts

BORN UNDER PUNCHES (IN BILLINGS, MONTANA)

welcome to the white
literary arts festival:
be palatable, tasty, even
be legible—yes this is one
of those poems about
disciplinary relegation,
circulation,
certitude

you ask for tea,
preferably Red Rose,
but they give you coffee.
just what you wanted:
stained-yellow teeth
barking histories of violence
jittery utterances of accusal
how embarrassing:
at least suck
on a breath mint
when you belch your miseries,
Crest Whitestrips
would go a long way

a "question" from the audience
an appeal to objectivity—
"account for yourself"
(i.e., count yourself
among the grateful
ndns to exist
in this space)

count yourself lucky
to exist
generally
but also
count yourself—
the Bureau of Indian Affairs
would like to know
where/when/what
you are

sit at the back of the room
by the garbage can
during the introduction of
"our esteemed authors"
this place was yours
long before you arrived here
detritus
but now your work can
keep you company.
company is hard
to keep
in spaces
like these

welcome to the white
literary arts festival,
there's a swag bag
in your hotel room
addressed to you
please find included:
a PowerBar
a poster

two candles
and a local review of
your book,
title misspelled
the worst image of you
on the planet accompanying,
and an ad to attend your
event: "best Indigenous artist"—
he's delighted to be here,
we promise,
even if
it hurts

My couch is a bed of pencils:
Is there such a thing as
writing back to legibility?
or rallying against consumption
in Indigenous literary studies?
Every time I write "kôhkom,"
some settler, somewhere,
cums. And when I say "tuguy,"
this same settler smiles
to themself, having
mastered the vernacular,
hung around the edges just
enough to be in the know,
titillated and satiated. the vibrancy
of ndn life on display is endlessly
knowable, learnable, it's unimaginable
that there's more going on beneath the
surface, that there are
whole economies of
care and relation that
are imperceptible,
nonsensical and, because of this,
illegible. I'll tell you a story:
my kôhkom (please control yourself)
and nikâwiy worked at a downtown
restaurant in Edmonton named the Cecil.
It was near the rathole, a since-demolished car tunnel—
now both no longer exist. While nikâwiy waited on customers
and cockroaches skittered across basement walls,
I'd sit patiently awaiting a breakfast my kôhkom

somehow found the time to prepare for me as
the kitchen was slammed with orders. She'd hand
the meal she prepared over to my mother to deliver
to my chubby, grubby hands, or would scuttle out of
the kitchen herself, arthritis endeavouring
but ultimately failing to slow her down.
I know that acts of care and love
are supposed to be noisy
declarations, to draw attention to both
the recipient and giver of love, but I also
know we didn't have a lot of food at home,
so my grandmother would hide pieces of bacon
under the pancakes she had
made for me, so if the manager walked by
she or my mother wouldn't get in trouble,
and my belly would be that much fuller
that day. I think about these intimate
acts of care, of getting on in the world,
obsessively. I don't care how much you
know about ndns, or which stories or words
you decide to take and which to leave,
because I remember how full my belly felt
from that borrowed bacon, and yes,
how full I felt from my kôhkom's
rickety love.

NARRATIVE TRAP(PING)

the protagonist,
bloodied, spent,
looks out
across the ocean,
to the sunset,
a sunset, any
sunset, with
an Indigenous
fleshy body
wounded, beside them
on the beach sands.

before the cut
to darkness
to black
to the credits,
the settler protagonist,
gazing
intently toward
the horizon,
has a brain
aneurysm,
dying
instantly
the Indigenous guide
sits on the beach
alive
help heard
in the offing
in the distance.

a group of
coded-Indigenous
supporting characters help
a carful
of white settlers
back to their
desires,
desired
stop, dodging
a menacing menagerie
of antagonists,
cronies
wishing painful death
upon
them, demise,
the intimidating antagonists
that wish
them ill,
violence.

on the way
back to the city
the car engine
catches
fire
and eventually
explodes,
the Indigenous
characters,
former
plot devices,
bear witness

from
a safe distance,
ride in another direction,
leaving a
flaming metal
car frame,
steel scaffolding
in their wake,
car horn
blaring,
heard for
miles.

just two
of endless
examples:
this is how
easy it is to
write a Hollywood
ending full
of live
ndns

COMMON SPACES

a hard truth
no one
prepares you
for: that you can
meet someone too
late in life

that foreclosures happen
where embers linger,
hold hope, spill over,
burn out. you feel every
extinguishing fire,
every flame limply
cherry and fade

i think a lot of poems
are about this, just
dressed up differently:
form obscures,
language obfuscates,
but longing clarifies,
longing sharpens,
while stealing focus,
until all you have
is something pure
and painful:
yearning

desire is
a struggling river,
mud-clogged inclines,
the largest couch
in the world,
a makeshift house
of want,
a laugh like
an echo that
rings out through
time and space,
like sugar,
constant humming
so it's hard to shake,
but especially when
you won't loosen
your grip
you think you're
above it, and yet
you're writing a
love poem at
age XX—
you'll call it
a love poem
on the one hand,
and disavow it
as such later

but longing
knows
when you're
a liar
when you're
trying to keep
afloat,
when desire is
a struggling river

my kôhkom's tongue cuts through the air like a helicopter blade thrumming acerbic nursery mobile a bed fit to curse you with a spell no roadside crystals can remedy a burial ground full of hipster dream-catcher tattoos & smudge kits bought off Amazon for $19.99 the cure for existential angst not for sale here vituperative stones fall from round mouths looking for gemstones millstones she'll let you gawk as long as you drown while you do it

KÔHKOM FREEDOM

for nikâwiy

freedom is selecting the
premium cable bundle
even though you can't
afford it,
and even
though all you
watch are the film
channels and TLC,
falling asleep to
John Hughes
movie marathons
or reruns of
*90 Day
Fiancé*

freedom is when
the low-fuel
light shines
bright on
your dash-
board,
but you
drive
to work
anyway,
lifting your
foot off the
gas

pedal as
you careen
downhill,
momentum
carrying you
forward

freedom is a phone
bill that will
never be
paid, but
you call
your niece
anyway,
to see if
she'll come
over to visit,
gossip
and mop
your floors
for twenty
dollars

freedom is a bingo
dabber that
never runs out,
because
when it
does
you remove
the top
and

pour
coffee in,
to mix
with
the ink

freedom is a debt
you can't escape
yet you charge
another Slurpee
to your overdraft
debit
card 'cause
it's sizzling
outside, and
blue
raspberry is
your favourite
flavour, and
they have
it this
time of
year (and
fuck them
anyway)

GLOSSARY

acimowin stories, storytelling
awâs go away
awâsisak children
kinanâskomitin thank you (singular)
kinanâskomitinâwâw thank you (plural)
kôhkom grandmother
mahihkan wolf
môniyâwak white people
nêhiyawêwin the Cree language
nîkânihk of the future
nôhkom nitânskotapân my great-grandmother
pîsim sun
wahkohtowin relationship, kinship

ACKNOWLEDGEMENTS

"Cree Dictionary" was originally published in *ndncountry*, a special co-produced issue of *Prairie Fire* (39.3) and *Contemporary Verse 2* (41.2) in fall 2018. It was also included in *Best Canadian Poetry 2019* (Biblioasis).

"Louise" was originally published in *Convergence*, a special issue of *Contemporary Verse 2* (40.1) in summer 2017.

"kinanâskomitin" was originally published in the *Malahat Review* (197) in winter 2017.

"Dancing Yellow Thunder" was originally published in the *Fieldstone Review* (9) in summer 2016.

"No Obvious Signs of Distress" was inspired by the story of Alan Ruel's arrest: https://www.cbc.ca/news/canada/calgary/rcmp-jail-cell-stroke-drunk-tank-1.5459539

"wahkohtowin" was originally published in *Contemporary Verse 2* (42.1) in summer 2019.

"150 Kilometres West of Saskatoon" was originally published with the title "150 kms west of Saskatoon" in *Arc Poetry* 84 in fall 2017.

"Stretch Marks // Sun Dogs" was originally published with the title "stretchmarks // sundogs" in *PRISM International* (57.1) in fall 2018.

"Woman Making Tea" was originally published in the *Capilano Review* (3.30) in fall 2016.

"A Prairie Fire That Wanders About" takes its title from the song by Sufjan Stevens.

"A Crook That Signifies Home" was originally published in *Eighteen Bridges* (11) in winter 2018.

"Born Under Punches (in Billings, Montana)" was originally published with the title "born under punches (in billings)" in the *Capilano Review* (42.3) in fall 2020. The poem takes its title from the song by Talking Heads.

"kôhkom Freedom" was originally published in the *Capilano Review* (42.3) in fall 2020.

This book of poetry is dedicated to my mother (nikâwiy), Pearl McRee.

I have also had the pleasure, opportunity, and good fortune to connect with numerous thinkers, writers, artists and poets over the years who have shaped my critical and creative process. While I can't name everyone, there are a few in particular who I have had the opportunity to read and think with (and alongside) who deserve special mention: Cecily Nicholson, Emily Riddle, Jessica Johns, Selina Boan, Mercedes Eng, Billy-Ray Belcourt, Samantha Nock, Jordan Abel, Richard Van Camp, Carleigh Baker, Rob Taylor, Gina Starblanket, Cole Nowicki, Sharon Stein, Tin Lorica, Savannah Todd, Marilyn Dumont, Lindsay Nixon, Conor McNally, Lianne Charlie, Arielle Twist, Jenny Heijun Wills, Brandi Bird, David Chariandy, Alicia Elliott, Kayla Czaga and Nickita Longman.

Profuse thanks to Emma, Silas and Amber for all their editorial work and support. Many thanks, additionally, to the Cree Land Mini Mart in Regina, Saskatchewan for the inspiration for the title of this book. If you're in the area, please do fill up there.

This book is a gesture to what it means to think otherwise about how we inhabit and relate to our homes. *CREELAND* is a space, a way of being, of living in and in relation to our homelands, full of joy, yet cognizant of myriad intimate violences. But, just as importantly, this book is about being steeped in love and community. hiy hiy!

ABOUT THE AUTHOR

Dallas Hunt is Cree and a member of Wapsewsipi (Swan River First Nation) in Treaty Eight territory in northern Alberta. He has had creative work published in *Contemporary Verse 2*, *Prairie Fire*, *PRISM International* and *Arc Poetry*. His first children's book, *Awâsis and the World-famous Bannock*, was published by Highwater Press in 2018 and was nominated for several awards. Hunt is an assistant professor of Indigenous literatures at the University of British Columbia.